Fairy Godmother's Diary

Retold by Frances Lee
Illustrated by Chantal Stewart

™ sundance
A Haights Cross Communications Company

Thursday

I've been watching Cinderella and her sisters. Those sisters are mean and bossy, and they yell at Cinderella all of the time.

"Cinders!" they scream. "Come and wash our hair!"

"Hurry up and sweep the floor!"

"When will our breakfast be ready?"

And she is always so nice to them! I must do something about it. I have a plan . . .

Friday morning

The first step in my plan has worked.
The Prince is having a ball, and I made sure
that an invitation was sent to Cinderella
and her sisters.

Poor Cinderella doesn't have a dress
to wear to the ball—but I'll fix that!

Friday afternoon

What a nasty pair those two are!
They are saying that Cinderella
has not been invited to the ball.
I'll make sure that she goes!

Saturday

Today I had great fun! The sisters went off to the ball early. They wanted to have a good look at the Prince and to get lots of food. Poor Cinderella was left at home alone.

All of a sudden, I appeared beside her. I waved my wand and changed her ragged clothes into a beautiful ball gown. I turned a pumpkin into a coach, some cats into servants, and some mice into horses.

Then I sent Cinderella to the ball. I warned her to be home by midnight because that was when my power would run out.

Sunday morning

Everyone is talking about the ball!
Cinderella was a great success.

The Prince danced with her all night.
The sisters were angry that he didn't
dance with them. And they didn't know
that Cinderella was the mystery princess!

Poor Cinderella was so happy dancing
with the Prince that she must have
forgotten the time. Just as the clock struck
twelve, she ran from the ball.

Monday evening

The Prince spent all day
searching for the mystery
princess. He found a glass
slipper that she had left behind.
He vowed that he would find
its owner and marry her.

The sisters were so excited.
The silly things thought that
the slipper might fit them.

When the Prince arrived,
the sisters smiled and bowed.
They squeezed and squeezed,
but they couldn't get their feet
into the slipper.

No way! Their feet were too big!

I made sure that the Prince saw Cinderella just as he was leaving. He insisted that she try on the slipper. It fit, of course!

The sisters were so angry! The Prince asked Cinderella to marry him, and he invited Cinderella to the palace to meet the King and Queen.

Tuesday

I've just come from the wedding.
I didn't have to give Cinderella
a beautiful dress—she now has dozens
of them.

Cinderella is so kind!
She invited those two terrible
sisters to the wedding. And she
gave them seats up front,
near the King and Queen!

But I made sure that a bee stung
the sisters. They both had red
lumps on their noses.

Poor things!

Wednesday

I am pleased with the way things have
turned out. Cinderella and the Prince are
very happy. The sisters live at the palace,
but now they have to do their own work.

I'm wondering what to do next.
I might see what I can do for poor
Humpty Dumpty. I hear that he had
a great fall!